Surrender at Appomattox

by Andrew Santella

Content Adviser: Patrick Schroeder, Historian,
Appomattox Court House National Historical Park

Reading Adviser: Susan Kesselring, M.A.,
Literacy Educator,
Rosemount-Apple Valley-Eagan (Minnesota) School District

COMPASS POINT BOOKS
MINNEAPOLIS, MINNESOTA

Compass Point Books
3109 West 50th Street, #115
Minneapolis, MN 55410

Visit Compass Point Books on the Internet at *www.compasspointbooks.com*
or e-mail your request to *custserv@compasspointbooks.com*

On the cover: Keith Rocco's painting *Surrender Meeting*, which depicts Robert E. Lee's surrender to Ulysses S. Grant at Appomattox Court House, Virginia.

Photographs ©: National Park Service/Artist, Keith Rocco, cover, 27; Prints Old and Rare, back cover (far left); Library of Congress, back cover, 8, 9, 35; Bettmann/Corbis, 4, 25; MPI/Getty Images, 6–7 (top), 10, 14, 18, 37; Appomattox Court House National Historical Park, 7 (bottom), 29, 34; North Wind Picture Archives, 11, 30, 33, 36; U.S. Senate Art Collection, *Ulysses S. Grant* by William F. Cogswell, 12; Stock Montage, Inc., 13; Corbis, 17, 20–21, 22; Hulton Archive/ Getty Images, 19, 31; The Granger Collection, New York, 28; Lee Snider/Photo Images/Corbis, 39; Joseph Sohm/ChromoSohm Inc./Corbis, 40.

Editor: Nick Healy
Page Production: The Design Lab
Photo Researcher: Marcie C. Spence
Cartographer: XNR Productions, Inc.
Library Consultant: Kathleen Baxter

Creative Director: Keith Griffin
Editorial Director: Carol Jones
Managing Editor: Catherine Neitge

Library of Congress Cataloging-in-Publication Data
Santella, Andrew.
  Surrender at Appomattox / by Andrew Santella.
     p. cm.—(We the people)
  Includes bibliographical references and index.
  ISBN 0-7565-1626-9 (hardcover)
  ISBN 0-7565-1766-4 (paperback)
  1. Appomattox Campaign, 1865—Juvenile literature. I. Title. II. We the people (Series)
(Compass Point Books)
  E477.67.S26 2005
  973.7'38—dc22   2005025064

TABLE OF CONTENTS

A LONG AND BLOODY WAR

Wilmer McLean had seen enough of the Civil War. The war's first great battle was fought not far from his home. The armies of the North and South clashed in a fierce and horrible struggle. McLean hoped he would never have to witness another.

Union and Confederate troops in combat at Manassas Junction, Virginia

When McLean was younger, he had served in the Virginia militia. But he had reached an age where he wanted only to live in peace and run his business. He was a merchant and the manager of a plantation. He made his home with his family near the little Virginia crossroads of Manassas Junction. It was there that the armies of the North and South met in the summer of 1861. The bloody fight is best known as the Battle of Bull Run.

Several months had passed since 11 Southern states had seceded from the Union. Differences over slavery and other issues had divided the nation. The Southern Confederacy aimed to form its own separate nation. Union troops from the North fought to hold the United States together as one.

At the Civil War's start, many people figured the Southern rebellion would not last long. The Confederates had notched an early victory by driving Union troops out of Fort Sumter in South Carolina. But the Union Army soon went on the move to defeat Confederate troops in

A chain of wagons hauling supplies to troops at Manassas

northern Virginia. Northerners were sure the Union Army would be successful and the war would be over.

As it turned out, the battle was fought near Wilmer McLean's property in Manassas, along a creek called Bull Run. Generals from the Confederate Army rented McLean's house for their headquarters. During the fighting, a cannonball crashed through his kitchen, which was in a separate building near the main house.

When the shooting finally stopped, the Confederate Army had driven the Union forces back in a stunning

victory. But both armies suffered heavy losses. About 4,700 men were killed, wounded, or captured on both sides. Suddenly, people understood this would be a long and bloody war. And fighting would soon return to Manassas. A second major battle took place there in August 1862.

After that, McLean moved away. He wanted to sell supplies to the Confederate Army, but he could not do it from northern Virginia. Manassas was

Wilmer McLean

often behind Union lines as the North and South battled for control of the region. He chose to make his new home in a tiny village in the far southern reaches of Virginia. The name of the village was Appomattox Court House. He figured he could do business without interference there.

McLean moved his family into a handsome brick house with a wide porch. He expected to find peace there.

The village of Appomattox Court House, Virginia

Wilmer McLean's home and the site of a closing chapter in the Civil War

But the Civil War would make its way once more to his front door. In fact, the last major act of the brutal conflict would be played out inside his home.

GRANT AND LEE

The Civil War was the deadliest conflict in United States history. Fighting stretched across much of the eastern half of the continent and lasted for four years. More than 620,000 people died as a result of the war.

Columbia, South Carolina, lay in ruins after the defeat of Confederate troops there.

Robert E. Lee on his favorite horse, Traveller

Southern states suffered much of the war's destruction. Most of the battles took place in the South, and by 1865 Union armies had seized much of the region. The Union wanted to reduce the South's will and ability to fight on. Northern troops destroyed railroads. They

General Ulysses S. Grant

burned plantations and farms. And their attacks left some of the South's biggest cities in ruins. Still, the people of the South and their leaders continued fighting. At the start of 1865, Confederate armies battled the Union in Virginia, Texas, the Carolinas, and elsewhere.

The people of the South largely placed their hopes in the army led by General Robert E. Lee. Lee's force was called the Army of Northern Virginia, and in battle after battle, it had frustrated larger Union forces. But in April 1865, Lee's army faced its most serious test yet.

A Union army led by General Ulysses S. Grant threatened Richmond, the capital of the Confederate States

of America. With more than 120,000 soldiers, Grant's forces outnumbered Lee's two to one. Grant's army had one other big advantage. The factories and railways of the North kept the Union armies well supplied with the weapons and clothing they needed.

The South had advantages of its own. Confederate troops were fighting on their home turf. They were surrounded by country they knew well and by a supportive public. They needed fewer troops to defend a location than their enemies would need to seize it. But for Lee, keeping his troops fed, clothed, and armed was a constant worry. Union forces had cut off

Jefferson Davis

The center of Richmond burned during the city's fall to Union troops.

the supply lines that Lee's troops depended on. Still, Lee was determined to find a way to win. "If defeated, nothing will be left for us to live for," he wrote.

14

On the first two days in April 1865, Grant's army launched attacks that sent the Confederates reeling into retreat. Confederate President Jefferson Davis and the rest of the Confederate government had to flee Richmond.

Lee and his army moved west and south of the city, fighting off Union attacks. Some of Lee's soldiers gave up. More and more began dropping their rifles and simply heading for home. General John B. Gordon described the retreat: "On and on, hour after hour, from hilltop to hilltop, the lines were alternately forming, fighting and retreating, making one almost continuous shifting." He also recalled, "There came running at the top of his speed a boy soldier." When asked why he was running, the soldier shouted back, "I'm running, 'cause I can't fly."

Still, Lee was determined to hold his army together. He believed he saw a way out of this trouble.

LEE'S LAST FIGHT

Lee's plan was to race his army southwest toward Danville, Virginia. Railroads in that area could bring supplies to his troops. Also he could join forces with another Confederate army there.

Lee's troops, however, were tired and desperately hungry. With the Union Army at their heels, the soldiers had little chance to sleep. Many of them had gone days without eating because their rations had run out. And soldiers were not the only ones going hungry. Armies of the 1800s depended on horses to pull wagons and haul cannons. Unable to find grain or grass, Lee's horses were sometimes too weak to work.

Everywhere they turned, the Confederates seemed to run into more Union soldiers. When their retreat was cut off near the village of Jetersville, they changed direc-tion and headed west toward Lynchburg. They hoped to get around the Union positions and then turn south. But

16

The remains of an ammunition train destroyed by Union troops

Grant followed close behind. On April 6, Union forces

caught up with a part of Lee's army and captured about

8,000 Confederate soldiers. When he learned what had

17

Some of Lee's retreating troops surrendered at Sayler's Creek, Virginia, where the Union Army caught up to them.

happened, Lee cried out, "My God! Has the army been dissolved?"

An officer watching the Confederate retreat wrote: "[T]he few men who still carried their muskets had hardly the appearance of soldiers … their clothes all tattered and covered with mud, their eyes sunken and lusterless … waiting for General Lee to say where they were to face about and fight."

The following day, Grant sent a rider carrying a flag of truce toward the Confederate lines. According to the rules of war, armies could send messages under white flags without fear of being attacked. Grant had written Lee a note urging him to surrender. "The results of the last week must convince you of the hopelessness of further resistance," Grant wrote. He asked Lee "to surrender that portion of the C.S. [Confederate States] army known as the Army of Northern Virginia."

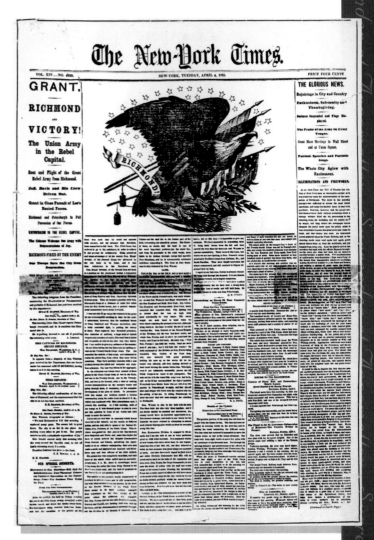

Headlines in The New York Times *celebrated Northern victories and Lee's retreat.*

Lee wrote back and told Grant that he wasn't yet ready to surrender. When he got the message, Grant turned to one of his officers and said, "It looks like Lee means to fight."

On April 8, some of Grant's forces moved into position to block Lee's path. The next day, Lee tried one last desperate attack. He sent his army to meet the Union forces near Appomattox Court House. But more hard-marching Union infantry arrived to support the troops already blocking Lee's line of retreat. The Confederates

Confederate troops retreated over the Appomattox River on the Pocahontas Bridge.

were beaten back and nearly surrounded. Lee had to face the fact that it was time to give up.

Some of Lee's officers tried to talk him out of surrendering. They suggested that the soldiers could take to the woods and mountains and fight as guerrillas—soldiers who use surprise tactics rather than the methods of traditional warfare. Lee rejected the idea. He knew it would only prolong the war and bring more misery to the South. "The enemy's cavalry would pursue [the Southern guerillas] and overrun many sections they may never have occasion to

visit. We would bring on a state of affairs it would take this country years to recover from."

There was only one course of action. "There is nothing left for me to do but go and see General Grant, and I would rather die a thousand deaths," he said. He sent

Confederate soldiers lay dead after being overrun by Union troops.

Grant a note offering to surrender. Grant had been suffering from a terrible headache. But when he received Lee's letter, the pain vanished. Grant wrote back that he would ride forward to meet with Lee. Taking a few aides, he rushed toward the front lines.

Meanwhile, Lee sent his aide, Lieutenant Colonel Charles Marshall, to find a suitable place to meet Grant. He headed for the village of Appomattox Court House.

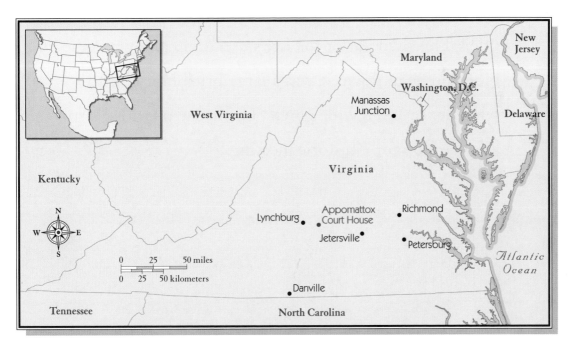

Robert E. Lee's retreat finally led to the village of Appomattox Court House.

It was a tiny settlement of about 20 buildings. The village held a dozen or so homes, some small shops, a tavern, and the Appomattox County Courthouse.

As Marshall rode through town, he encountered Wilmer McLean. More than two years had passed since McLean bought his home in Appomattox. Marshall asked McLean if he knew where General Lee could hold an important meeting. At first, McLean tried to direct the officer to an unfurnished building, but eventually McLean offered his own parlor for Lee's use. McLean owned the nicest home in town. It was a large brick house, with a white fence and a wide porch. The house provided a suitable location for a historic meeting.

THE GENERALS MEET

Even though Lee had agreed to surrender, important questions had to be addressed. Would Lee and the rest of his army become Grant's prisoners? Would they be considered traitors? Would they be punished for taking

Ulysses S. Grant enters the McLean house to meet Robert E. Lee.

part in the war? The meeting between Grant and Lee would answer those questions. In military language, this was known as stating the terms of surrender.

Lee arrived first and waited anxiously in McLean's parlor. He was dressed in a fancy new uniform, with a sash and a sword. "I have probably to be General Grant's prisoner, and I thought I must make my best appearance," he explained to an aide.

Grant arrived 30 minutes after Lee. He was dressed in a regular officer's sack coat and pants. He carried no sword. His pants and boots were muddy from his long ride. The two generals shook hands and sat down about 10 feet (3 meters) apart from each other. After a few minutes of conversation, Lee asked Grant to write out the terms of surrender. Grant wrote out a short note, and handed it to Lee to read. It stated that the Confederates would be free to go home, as long as they promised not to continue fighting. The Confederates would not be taken to prison camps or treated as traitors.

Lee asked about one detail that was not covered in Grant's written terms. He understood that his soldiers would have to hand over their weapons and other military goods, but he wondered about their horses. In many cases, the horses belonged to the soldiers themselves, not the Confederate Army. Could Lee's soldiers keep their horses?

Grant said that they could. He knew the soldiers would need them to rebuild their farms and homes. "The

Generals Grant and Lee meet to discuss terms of surrender for Lee's army.

Robert E. Lee signs the terms of his army's surrender.

country has been so raided by the two armies, it is doubtful whether they will be able to put in a crop to carry themselves and their families though the next winter" without their horses, Grant later wrote.

Lee was pleased with Grant's generous treatment. "This will have the best possible effect upon the men," he said.

After Lee signed the papers, he stood to shake hands with the Northern officers. One of them was a Native American from the Seneca nation named Ely Parker. Lee apparently noticed Parker and said, "I'm glad to see one real American here." Parker is said to have responded, "We are all Americans."

Ely Parker

One of the Union officers said to Grant, "This will live in history." But the general was in no mood to celebrate. He later wrote, "My own feelings … were sad and depressed at the downfall of a foe who had fought so long and valiantly, and had suffered so much for a cause, though that cause was, I believe, one of the worst for which a people ever fought."

AFTER THE FIGHTING

News of the surrender spread quickly. One of the first messages Grant sent was to the War Department in Washington, D.C.: "General Lee surrendered the Army of Northern Virginia this afternoon on terms proposed by

General Lee leaving the McLean house after his surrender

myself." In Washington, joyful crowds took to the streets to celebrate and wave flags. "The air seemed to burn with the bright hues of the flag," wrote one reporter.

Among the soldiers of the Union Army, the celebration was even wilder. "Thank God Lee has surrendered," a soldier named Elisha Rhodes wrote in his journal. "Sometime in the afternoon, we heard loud cheering at the front, and soon Major General Meade commanding the Army of the Potomac rode like mad down the road with his hat off, shouting, 'The war is over and we are going home!' Such a scene only happens once in centuries. … I cried and laughed by turns. I was never so happy in my life."

General George Meade

At the McLean house, soldiers hunted for souvenirs of the historic meeting. They bought—or stole—some of the furniture from McLean's parlor. Union troops began firing their guns into the air in celebration, but Grant ordered them to stop. "The war is over. The rebels are our countrymen again," he told them. Out of concern for the starving soldiers of Lee's army, Grant ordered 25,000 rations sent across the lines to them. For some of the Confederates, this would be the first food they had eaten in days.

Lee rode back from Appomattox Court House to find his troops lining the road with their hats off as a sign of respect for him. They cheered as Lee passed. "I love you just as well as ever, General Lee," said one soldier. Others could not accept the defeat. "Grim, bearded men threw themselves on the ground ... and wept like children," one officer remembered. Lee stopped to tell some of his soldiers, "I have done the best I could for you."

Even with Lee's surrender, the war was not officially over. Other Confederate armies remained in the

Robert E. Lee says farewell to troops after surrendering at Appomattox.

field, and they were not bound to Lee's action. His surrender was just for the Army of Northern Virginia. Some Confederates remained determined to fight. The war could have dragged on much longer. But no one in the South was more respected than Robert E. Lee. Most Southerners followed his lead and gave up the struggle. (The war officially ended on May 10, 1865, one month after Lee's surrender.)

Confederate soldiers were issued parole passes to ensure their safe return home.

Grant and Lee met one more time at Appomattox. The day after his surrender, Lee asked Grant if he would provide Southern soldiers some kind of proof that they were paroled prisoners. Lee did not want his men arrested or imprisoned on their way home. Grant agreed. Over the next few days, the Union Army printed 28,231 parole certificates for the defeated Confederates.

The official surrender ceremony for the infantry was conducted April 12, 1865. About 25,000 Confederate soldiers marched in formation before their Union counterparts. Troops from each side saluted each other as a final show of respect. One by one, Southern units stepped for-

Northern and Southern troops gathered for an official surrender ceremony.

ward to stack their rifles and other weapons. Then they folded up and surrendered their prized battle flags, which had been carried through years of war. "Was this to be the end of all our marching and fighting for the past four years? I could not keep back the tears," one soldier wrote.

With the fighting over, the task ahead was to reunite a country divided by years of bitter war. With their actions

President Lincoln speaks outside the White House.

at Appomattox, Grant and Lee showed the nation that former enemies could put aside their differences.

But the aftermath of the Civil War was not always peaceful. In a speech in Washington on April 11, President Abraham Lincoln described his plans for rebuilding the South and restoring the Union. Listening to the speech was a Southerner named John Wilkes Booth. "That is the last speech he will ever make," he vowed. Three days later, Booth shot and killed Lincoln.

REMEMBERING APPOMATTOX

In four long years of fighting, hundreds of thousands lost their lives. But the war preserved the Union, and it secured the freedom of 4 million African-American slaves. The surrender at Appomattox signaled the end of

A sketch of Appomattox Court House as it looked in 1866

37

the war. It also showed how the two sides could put aside the bitterness of war and come together as citizens of one nation. Still, it would be years before the wounds of the Civil War were healed.

After playing his small part in the historic surrender, Wilmer McLean moved once again. His home in the village of Appomattox Court House was purchased by new owners. Almost 30 years later, the owners made plans to relocate the house to Washington, D.C., where it would be rebuilt and used as a Civil War museum. The house was dismantled, but the plans fell through before it could be moved to the nation's capital. For many years, the house lay in pieces in the Virginia countryside. Planks of wood rotted away. Many bricks were taken by souvenir seekers, but more than 5,500 original bricks were used in reconstructing the home.

The entire village of Appomattox Court House fell into poor condition after the war. At first, the site was not of great interest to veterans and groups who wanted to

The parlor of the rebuilt McLean house

honor the history of the Civil War. After all, the village

had not been the location of a great battle. Neither the

North nor the South hurried to build a monument there or

to preserve the buildings.

That changed with time, and the U.S. Congress

finally acted to preserve the site of Grant and Lee's

39

The McLean house is part of a national historical park.

historic meeting. In 1935, Congress created the Appomattox Court House Historical Monument at the site of the McLean house, to preserve the memory of the surrender. Archeologists began digging at the homesite, looking for clues about life in the 1800s. By 1949, builders had created a careful restoration of the McLean House and other village buildings, and opened them to the public.

Today, more than 150,000 people visit the site—now known as the Appomattox Court House National Historical Park—each year. They tour the restored McLean house and enjoy multimedia displays and historical reenactments.

The Civil War is remembered as the conflict that divided the nation for four long years. The home of Wilmer McLean in Appomattox Court House, Virginia, is remembered as the site where the United States began to become one again.

GLOSSARY

archeologists—scientists who study people, places, and things of the past

crossroads—a small settlement at the junction of two highways or roads

guerillas—soldiers who are not part of a country's regular army

infantry—soldiers trained to fight on foot

militia—an army of part-time soldiers

paroled—set free or released from a prison term

plantation—large farm in the South, usually worked by slaves

rations—food given to soldiers each day

seceded—withdrew from a group

DID YOU KNOW?

- Their meeting at Appomattox was not the first for Ulysses S. Grant and Robert E. Lee. They had met once before when both served in the U.S. Army during the Mexican War (1846–1848).

- The surrender terms set by Grant and Lee were sometimes called the Gentlemen's Agreement because both generals conducted their historic meeting with dignity and honor.

- President Abraham Lincoln toured Richmond, Virginia, the Confederate capital, on April 4, 1865, immediately after the city fell to Union forces.

- Captain Robert Todd Lincoln, the president's son, was among Grant's aides who were in the room when Lee surrendered.

IMPORTANT DATES

Timeline

1860	Abraham Lincoln is elected president on November 6.
1861	South Carolina secessionists launch attack on U.S. forces at Fort Sumter; First Battle of Bull Run (or Manassas) fought on July 21.
1862	Lincoln issues the Emancipation Proclamation, declaring the slaves free.
1865	Union troops occupy Richmond, Virginia, on April 2; General Robert E. Lee surrenders Army of Northern Virginia to General Ulysses S. Grant on April 9; Confederate troops parade and surrender arms on April 12.

IMPORTANT PEOPLE

ULYSSES S. GRANT (1822–1885)
Commander of Union forces during the Civil War and 18th president of the United States

ROBERT E. LEE (1807–1870)
Commander of the Confederate Army of Northern Virginia from June 1862 to April 1865

ABRAHAM LINCOLN (1809–1865)
Sixteenth president of the United States, who led the nation through the Civil War and freed the slaves

WANT TO KNOW MORE?

At the Library

Marrin, Albert. *Unconditional Surrender: U.S. Grant and the Civil War.*
New York: Atheneum, 1994.

McGowen, Tom. *Surrender at Appomattox.* New York: Children's Press, 2004.

Williams, Jean Kinney. *Ulysses S. Grant.* Minneapolis: Compass Point Books, 2003.

On the Web

For more information on the *Surrender at Appomattox*, use FactHound
to track down Web sites related to this book.

1. Go to *www.facthound.com*

2. Type in a search word related to this book
   or this book ID: 0756516269

3. Click on the *Fetch It* button.

Your trusty FactHound will fetch the best Web sites for you!

On the Road

Appomattox Court House
National Historical Park
Highway 24
Appomattox, VA 24522
Wilmer McLean's house and the
surrounding village restored to
their 1865 appearance

Manassas National Battlefield Park
12521 Lee Highway
Manassas, VA 20109
The site of the Civil War's first
great battle, also known as the Battle
of Bull Run

Look for more We the People books about this era:

The Assassination of Abraham Lincoln
ISBN 0-7565-0678-6

The Battle of Gettysburg
ISBN 0-7565-0098-2

Battle of the Ironclads
ISBN 0-7565-1628-5

The Carpetbaggers
ISBN 0-7565-0834-7

The Emancipation Proclamation
ISBN 0-7565-0209-8

Fort Sumter
ISBN 0-7565-1629-3

The Gettysburg Address
ISBN 0-7565-1271-9

Great Women of the Civil War
ISBN 0-7565-0839-8

The Lincoln–Douglas Debates
ISBN 0-7565-1632-3

The Missouri Compromise
ISBN 0-7565-1634-X

The Reconstruction Amendments
ISBN 0-7565-1636-6

The Underground Railroad
ISBN 0-7565-0102-4

A complete list of We the People titles is available on our Web site:
www.compasspointbooks.com

INDEX

About the Author

Andrew Santella writes for magazines and newspapers, including *GQ* and the *New York Times Book Review*. He is the author of a number of books for young readers. He lives outside Chicago with his wife and son.